Turning Around

Turning Around

Reflections, Questions, and Prayers for
the Days in the Season of Lent

ROBERT BOAK SLOCUM

RESECURCE *Publications* · Eugene, Oregon

Ash Wednesday

"Remember that you are dust, and to dust you shall return." (Ash Wednesday liturgy, BCP, p. 265)

It's scary, the reminder with imposition of ashes that dust is our mortal destination. Whoever we are, whatever we have, dust is where we "return." And yet the words at the imposition of ashes can spur us for real life. We can discover life that lives, life in God, if we can see beyond ourselves. Our life isn't all about *us*. We are not and cannot be the center of our world. If we live only in ourselves, if our trust is only for ourselves, our ultimate future is only dust, only death. But this Lent can be a time to see God in faith and share life that's more than dust. Ash Wednesday points beyond life that can only die.

?

Are your concerns and actions self-centered? Must you always come first? How does that feel? Do you find meaning beyond yourself? How does it feel to help someone else?

+

Deliver us, Lord, from selfishness. Deliver us from anxious self-concern, and pushing ourselves ahead of others. Save us, Lord, because we cannot save ourselves. Help us to give ourselves to others as you give yourself to us.

Thursday after Ash Wednesday

> "Then Jesus told his disciples, 'If any want to become my followers, let them deny themselves and take up their cross and follow me.'" (Matt 16:24)(NRSV)

The devotions and disciplines of Lent can help us to give ourselves away in love for God, for others, and all creation. We abandon ourselves in God's love and offer ourselves as we share divine love generously. We can forgive others as we have been forgiven. We can reach out to others as we know God is constantly with us and claims us. It helps if we can sacrifice and release our own agenda, our insistence on having our desires and expectations met without consideration of others.

The disciplines of Lent can give us some practice and help us make needed changes to remove obstacles and share God's love. But the changes are not an ultimate end in themselves. If chocolate, or food in general, or drink has become an obstacle for your relationship with God or living a full life of faith, Lent is a good time to make some changes in those areas. But Lent is much more than a self-improvement program, a time to slim here or strengthen there. Instead we may wonder how to open our hearts more fully, know our Lord more nearly, give our life for Christ's sake entirely. This can begin with the next step we take.

?

What does it mean for you to take up your cross? Is this something new for you today, or something you have carried for a long time? Are you approaching your cross differently during this Lent? Will you take something on or leave something off? Are there obstacles between you and God? Are there obstacles between you and the life you want to live? Can you remove or reduce those obstacles? Are you approaching your obstacles differently during this Lent? What can you change?

+

Help us, Lord, to take up our cross daily and follow you. Help us to remove or change any obstacle that comes between us. Help us to know you better.

Friday after Ash Wednesday

> "When [the prodigal son] came to himself he said, 'How many of my father's hired hands have bread enough and to spare, but here I am dying of hunger! I will get up and go to my father, and I will say to him, 'Father, I have sinned against heaven and before you; I am no longer worthy to be called your son; treat me like one of your hired hands.'" (Luke 15:17–19)(NRSV)

Conversion is a turning around. The prodigal son literally changed the direction of his life when he faced what he did and returned home. No excuses, no rationalizations, no blaming someone else. He came clean and went home to start over in the lowest place. He trusted his father's mercy. It was a time to make things right. He took the first steps.

Lent can be our time to make things right. We can turn around with God's help. We can make a new start and improve the direction of our lives. We can trust in God's merciful grace. We can let go of our excuses and rationalizations. We can come to terms with who we are and where we're going. We can admit and repent what we did wrong, we can accept the forgiving grace that God freely provides and move forward with new direction. We can also forgive the people in our life who have hurt us, and accept the forgiveness of those we have hurt. We can heal and accept new life.

?

Do you need to turn around in some area of your life? Can you take responsibility for things you need to change? Can you accept the vulnerability of admitting when you were at fault and asking for forgiveness? Can you forgive yourself? Can you recognize where you were not at fault and where you did the best you could under the circumstances? Can you forgive others when needed and let it go? Can you take steps to protect yourself and others from harm? Can you trust that God still loves you and seeks the best for you?

+

Merciful God, forgive us and help us to forgive others who hurt us. Help us accept your forgiveness and the welcome you offer us. Help us share your love in the world. Help us to give and forgive.

Saturday after Ash Wednesday

"So [the prodigal son] set off and went to his father. But while he was still far off, his father saw him and was filled with compassion; he ran and put his arms around him, and kissed him. . . [T]he father said to his slaves, 'Quickly, bring out a robe—the best one—and put it on him; put a ring on his finger and sandals on his feet. And get the fatted calf and kill it, and let us eat and celebrate; for this son of mine was dead and is alive again; he was lost and is found!' And they began to celebrate." (Luke 15:20, 22–24)(NRSV)

Lent is a time for reconciliation. We may draw back from the thought of reconciliation because it seems so improbable, and hard on our pride to admit our part in an estrangement or misunderstanding. Of course, it takes both sides of a disagreement to share a full reconciliation, and we have no control over the other. But sometimes reconciliation may be easier than we would have imagined. We can take the first step. We can at least do our part to make reconciliation possible, and see how the other responds. The prodigal son just needed to show up, ask, and accept the wonderful generosity of his father's forgiveness. He was welcomed, loved, and embraced. There was no scolding or recrimination from his father. There was reconciliation and celebration. The prodigal son was home. He could make a new start. They could make a new start together.

?

Do you need to reconcile with someone? Can you forgive and accept forgiveness? What stands in the way and what can you do about it? Would it help to let go of anger, resentment, and pride? Can you celebrate a reconciliation?

+

Loving God, help us remove the barriers that prevent us from knowing you and each other. Forgive us, and help us to forgive. Be patient with us, and help us to be patient with others. O Lord, help us to make room for you in our lives, and help us to make room for others. Let us share your love.

Sunday, Lent 1

> "But [the older brother] answered his father, 'Listen! For all these years I have been working like a slave for you, and I have never disobeyed your command; yet you have never given me even a young goat so that I might celebrate with my friends. But when this son of yours came back, who has devoured your property with prostitutes, you killed the fatted calf for him.' Then the father said to him, 'Son, you are always with me, and all that is mine is yours. But we had to celebrate and rejoice, because this brother of yours was dead and has come to life; he was lost and has been found.'" (Luke 15:29–32)

It's not fair! If you've ever lived in a house with siblings you've probably heard "it's not fair!" Someone got too much or too little. One got to do something the other couldn't do, or one had to do something the other avoided. And on and on. Sometimes there can be too much fairness and not enough love.

The fairness issue was clear in the Gospel parable of the prodigal son. The older son had it right if we look at what happened from his narrow perspective of fairness. The older son did everything he was supposed to do. He was responsible from first to last. The younger son disappeared and wasted everything he was given. And then the big celebration was in honor of the *younger* son! Frankly, it *wasn't* fair. But it was good.

The celebration was for the younger son's *life* which was lost but found at last. The loving father of both brothers treated his younger son better than he deserved. The father met the younger son on his way home with a loving welcome. The father lavishly provided his returning son with gifts and a celebration of new life. That's how God treats us. Better than we deserve.

It helps if we follow the younger son's steps and turn around when we're going the wrong way. It helps if we accept God's amazing and abundant gifts that exceed our imagination or deserving. We may discover God has a party prepared for us. It also helps if we treat others better than they deserve.

?

Have you ever been jealous? Did you wish someone else's good fortune or success was *yours*? Can you appreciate another's moment of joy? Have you been able to offer something another person really needed? Did you share something that made a difference?

+

Most generous God, help us share ourselves with others. Help us offer our gifts, our time, and love. Help us to be with others. Let us celebrate their times of joy and stand close in their challenging times. Let us draw near to them as you are close to us, and know us well.

Monday, Lent 1

> Jesus said, "A man had two sons; he went to the first and said, 'Son, go and work in the vineyard today.' He answered, 'I will not'; but later he changed his mind and went. The father went to the second and said the same; and he answered, 'I go sir'; but he did not go. Which of the two did the will of his father?'" (Matt 21:28b-31) (NRSV)

Our words are important but our actions speak louder. Kind thoughts and good intentions in a time of crisis may not be nearly enough when we can *act* to make a difference. Best wishes can be hollow if we only offer words when our actions could help in a time of real need. The starving cannot eat our words, but they would greatly appreciate the food and water we share. We may be called to offer more than "thoughts and prayers"—unless we see that our actions can be *prayers in action.*

Despite his initial unwillingness, it was the first son in the parable who did his father's will. The second son's actions didn't match his words of obedience. His behavior warns us of the fraud that's possible when actions belie words.

Words allow us wonderful expression of our inmost thoughts and feelings. Words allow us to share with others, communicating and sharing our values and everything that matters to us. But every day we need to align our actions and words with care. Sometimes we fail miserably. Sometimes our intentions are good but we miss the mark. We can admit when our words and actions diverged, and we can be attentive to remove contradictions between them. We can be authentic. Grace and forgiveness make it possible.

?

Have there been times when your words and actions went in different directions? Did your actions belie your words? Did you contradict yourself? Were your words good but your actions insufficient? Did your words fail to express or reflect the truth of your actions? What can you do to better align your actions and words?

+

Give us courage, Lord, to speak our truth and live it. Strengthen our voice to tell of your love; make us strong to share your love in our lives. Help us find our salvation in you. Help us to know it and speak it and show it.

Tuesday, Lent 1

Jesus said, "'A man was going down from Jerusalem to Jericho, and fell into the hands of robbers, who stripped him, beat him, and went away, leaving him half dead. Now by chance a priest was going down that road; and when he saw him, he passed by on the other side. So likewise a Levite, when he came to the place and saw him, passed by on the other side. But a Samaritan while traveling came near him; and when he saw him, he was moved with pity. He went to him and bandaged his wounds, having poured oil and wine on them. Then he put him on his own animal, brought him to an inn, and took care of him.'" (Luke 10:30–34)(NRSV)

Going out of our way to help can seem to be such an inconvenience. It breaks up the day. It distracts us from important plans, interrupts our agenda. Our intentions may be good, but we may be reluctant to take the first step. And yet our most important opportunity today may be unexpected and demand flexibility. Perhaps we can step outside our comfort zone and still be safe.

The priest and the Levite took steps out of the way to avoid the badly injured traveler. They had no time for him. The officially religious people in this parable had agendas of their own that didn't include a stranger's unexpected emergency and need. Their actions didn't reflect the faith they claimed. Fortunately for the injured traveler, help came from a surprising source—a *Samaritan* who was good. Samaritans were not highly regarded in the Judaism of Jesus' day.

Sometimes in Lent we may give something up or take something on to draw nearer to God. These simple practices can be a token first step for an offer of our lives, a new way of life. The Samaritan made another person's troubles his own concern. He let go of his plans and a good bit of his time, energy, and money to help. In Jesus' day, the hearer of this parable would also likely have to let go of his prejudice against Samaritans to appreciate the story. Unexpected needs can help us discover what we should do and what we need to quit.

?

Will you sacrifice during this Lent? Will this sacrifice lead to change and transformation for a life that is more whole and more holy? Or is it just a token? Is there a sacrifice for you that will actually help you and others? Is there a sacrifice that leads to healing, hope, renewal, important sharing? Can you take something on or let something go in a way that draws you closer to God and others?

+

God of all mercies, help us find our way to you. Renew us; make us new in your love. And help us respond with our lives. Let us give back, remove obstacles, and grow into the life you offer. Shape us, and help us shape our lives in love with you.

Wednesday, Lent 1

> Jesus said, "[W]hoever does not take up the cross and follow me is not worthy of me. Those who find their life will lose it, and those who lose their life for my sake will find it." (Matt 10:38–39)(NRSV)

The cross is an instrument of sacrifice. For Jesus, the cross was his final mortal sacrifice. On the cross he gave his life for us and our salvation. Many of Jesus' disciples followed his way to their own ultimate sacrifice and death. But the way of the cross has many paths. We may not find ourselves nailed to a wooden cross or in other ways martyred for Christian faith. But we are invited by Jesus with all his followers to deny ourselves and take up our cross and follow him.

The cross separates us from everything that comes between us and God. Each person's cross is unique. In this Lent we can commit to removing our obstacles to living faith. We can begin to let go of our selfishness, our half-hearted use of our gifts, our jealousy and resentment, our fear of failing and unwillingness to try, our over-concern with what others may think. We can begin to let go of whatever obstructs faith. That will require sacrifices by us. Changing old habits can be difficult and sometimes painful. But it is possible with help from beyond us in God and with others who support us. We can take up our cross.

?

Is there something in your life that you want to change? Is there something that weighs you down, draws you off track, continues to disturb you, or gets in the way? Is there something like heavy luggage that you drag with you from place to place? Can you let go of it? Can you embrace the cross?

+

Lord of all hope, walk with me as I find new paths. Guide me on the way. Help me discover what I need and let go of anything that obstructs the way. Let me help others, and let others help me. Help me to lift my cross.

Thursday, Lent 1

> Jesus said, "So when you are offering your gift at the altar, if you remember that your brother or sister has something against you, leave your gift there before the altar and go; first be reconciled to your brother or sister, and then come and offer your gift." (Matt 5:23–24)(NRSV)

We can know God better through others, and express our love for God in the loving ways we treat others. Help given to the weakest and most vulnerable is help given to Jesus; and help denied to the weakest and most vulnerable is help denied to Jesus. Our Lord reminds us that we're in this life together with God and others. In the words of the Lord's Prayer, we pray to "our Father in heaven." We ask that God will "give us today our daily bread." In the Lord's Prayer we don't pray for God to "give *me* today *my* daily bread." We ask for God's help for *us*. Give us. Help us. Forgive us. Heal us. Lead us in the way we should go.

Jesus invites us to unity with God and each other. The Church's mission is "to restore all people to unity with God and each other in Christ" (BCP, p. 855). So a tear in the fabric of our unity with each other is serious: an obstacle to the fullness of life together with God and others, an obstacle to the unity we're created to enjoy. In our worship we pray for unity and celebrate its meaning for us. We contradict that unity when we hold grudges or avoid reconciliation. It's better to work for unity and reconciliation than to celebrate an ideal of unity that we deny by our actions. First be reconciled (at least try), and then offer your gift in celebration of the life we share with God.

?

How can we find common ground in a disagreement or separation from another? How can we identify what keeps us apart? Do you insist the other person take the first step to reconcile, or satisfy certain conditions before you will forgive? How does the forgiveness we receive from God and others relate to the forgiveness we offer those who hurt or disappoint us?

+

Lord of all hopefulness, help us to seek reconciliation with those who need to forgive us, and those we need to forgive. Draw us all together with grace and help us to be at one with you. Help us release our resentments and everything that stands between us and you. Show us how small are our aggravations and disagreements in the brilliant light of your love.

Friday, Lent 1

"As [Jesus] entered a village, ten lepers approached him. Keeping their distance, they called out, saying, 'Jesus, Master, have mercy on us!' When he saw them, he said to them, 'Go and show yourselves to the priests.' And as they went, they were made clean. Then one of them, when he saw that he was healed, turned back, praising God with a loud voice. He prostrated himself at Jesus' feet and thanked him. And he was a Samaritan. Then Jesus asked, 'Were not ten made clean? But the other nine, where are they? Was none of them found to return and give praise to God except this foreigner?' Then he said to him, 'Get up and go on your way; your faith has made you well.'" (Luke 17:12–19)(NRSV)

It's easy to take for granted the many gifts and blessings we have received and continue to enjoy. It's easy to presume that every success is our own doing; we've done it all ourselves. We may feel entitled and find it hard to imagine how our lives could have been otherwise. A perspective of thankfulness may help us recognize the many good things we've received, the blessings we've known, the support and help of others that have made a difference for us.

Jesus healed 10 but only one returned with thanks for an amazing and life-changing gift. *Be the person who thanks.* Be the one in 10.

Eucharist means thanksgiving, and at every service of the Eucharist we offer thanks for our creation, forgiveness, redemption, inspiration, and every gift. Remember and give thanks as you offer your gifts to others and at the altar. Forgive as you have been forgiven. Know you are loved, and love generously. Know you have been upheld, and find ways to uphold others. Give the benefit of a doubt and second chances when you can. The gifts we offer can be our thanksgiving.

?

Are you thankful? Have you taken gifts for granted, felt entitled to special favors, or forgotten to give thanks for the gifts you have received? When has another's help made a difference for you in recent days? What gifts have you received? How can you offer thanks, share generosity, and pay forward?

+

Generous and loving God, help us to recognize your gifts in our lives and respond with thanks. Help us celebrate the abundance of your love and live generously. Help us to be thankful for every good gift from friend or stranger. Let our thanks be offered in concern and appreciation for others and praise for you. May our love overflow. Let us know your generosity in our abundance of giving and receiving. Let our sharing draw us closer to each other and to you.

Saturday, 1 Lent

> At the Last Supper, Jesus said to his disciples "I give you a new commandment, that you love one another. Just as I have loved you, you also should love one another. By this everyone will know that you are my disciples, if you have love for one another." (John 13:34–35)(NRSV)

Living Christianity is a way of love, as Episcopal Presiding Bishop Michael Curry stated. Christianity is not just a system of thought to be understood or a code of laws to be obeyed. Jesus calls us to *love* one another as he loves us. It was once said of the early Christians, "see how they love one another." We will be known as Jesus' disciples when we have love for one another, and our love is visible. The love he invites us to share is not mere courtesy or politeness or tolerance but a willingness to give ourselves to the point of sacrifice. In this way we can become true friends who follow the way of love together. In this way we care for each other, watch out for each other, accept others' needs and concerns as our own, extend ourselves in love and generosity and friendship. Every day we discover opportunities to give and receive love in this communion of friends.

?

How does love make a difference in your life? When have you known it? How have you shown love for God, family, friends, strangers, the world? When have you been surprised by love? Do you sometimes block the flow of love in your life? How can you grow in love?

+

Lord of our hearts, help us to love you with all we are and all we have. Help us to love generously as you love us. Help us love the ones you love; help us love them all. Help us love your creation and care for it. Help us to give generously as we have received.

Sunday, Lent 2

"Jesus also told this parable to some who trusted in themselves that they were righteous and regarded others with contempt. 'Two men went up to the temple to pray, one a Pharisee and the other a tax collector. The Pharisee, standing by himself, was praying thus, "God, I thank you that I am not like other people: thieves, rogues, adulterers, or even like this tax collector. I fast twice a week; I give a tenth of all my income." But the tax collector, standing far off, would not even look up to heaven, but was beating his breast and saying, "God, be merciful to me, a sinner!" I tell you, this man went down to his home justified rather than the other; for all who exalt themselves will be humbled, but all who humble themselves will be exalted.'" (Luke 18:9–14)(NRSV)

Arrogant. The Pharisee was arrogant. He looked down on others who seemed so different from him, so inferior to him, even the person praying in the same temple. The Pharisee did all the right things but it went all wrong for him. He "checked every box" on the list of religious piety, but he couldn't see beyond himself. He missed the meaning of what he did. Instead of opening his heart to God and others, he only worshiped himself and his own apparent virtue. He was the supreme being and higher power in his own life, but he couldn't save himself. His pious practices were actually getting in the way of living faith. There was no room in his heart to receive God's help or share the tax collector's prayer for mercy. The Pharisee was stuck on himself.

It is God's grace that draws us to completion and we need to be on the way. Our faith is not a self-help project. Without God we're incomplete and stuck. Nothing less than God will do for our greatest need. We need to receive help from beyond ourselves to heal and grow. We open wide the door to grace as we look beyond ourselves and see the needs of others. As we share generously we may discover and receive surprising gifts.

?

Have you been arrogant? Have you felt better than others because of something you did? Do you deserve better treatment than others? Are you entitled to a superior position? Do you play by your own set of rules? What brings you back to your true self? What helps you see your need for help beyond yourself? How can you help and be helped by others? How can others help you find God in your life?

+

Dear Lord, help us know how much you love us. Help us know that we don't need to be puffed up; we don't need to inflate ourselves at the expense of others. Guide us to realize we don't need to prove ourselves to you, because you already know our every strength and every flaw. Help us see that we stand tallest when we bend to help or kneel to serve.

Monday, 2 Lent

> "Then [Jesus] told this parable: 'A man had a fig tree planted in his vineyard; and he came looking for fruit on it and found none. So he said to the gardener, 'See here! For three years I have come looking for fruit on this fig tree, and still I find none. Cut it down! Why should it be wasting the soil?' He replied, 'Sir, let it alone for one more year, until I dig around it and put manure on it. If it bears fruit next year, well and good; but if not, you can cut it down.'" (Luke 13:6–9)(NRSV)

The impatient landowner wanted the fig tree cut down from his vineyard because it bore no fruit. It seemed to be such a waste of space. But the gardener knew better. He gave the tree another chance to bear fruit. He had a plan for the tree in the next year with hope for a better result.

We may find a second chance this Lent. Another chance to turn around. Another chance to remove obstacles between us and God; another chance to remove the barriers and walls between ourselves and others. Another chance to share our love. God offers us mercy instead of anger. We have time to make a difference. We can accept the love, forgiveness, and inspiration that God provides us constantly. We can forgive others and accept their forgiveness; we can forgive ourselves. We can accept another chance.

?

When were you given a second chance? What happened? Who offered a second chance to you? A family member? A friend? God?

Did it make a difference for you? Have you offered second chances to others? What happened?

+

Most patient and loving God, forgive us as we forgive those who need our forgiveness. Give us your mercy. Help us use the time we have to turn around and renew our life in you. Help us to begin again, and stand whenever we fall. Help us to share second chances with others.

Tuesday, 2 Lent

> Jesus told this parable to the Pharisees and the scribes: "'Which one of you, having a hundred sheep and losing one of them, does not leave the ninety-nine in the wilderness and go after the one that is lost until he finds it? When he has found it, he lays it on his shoulders and rejoices.'" (Luke 15:2–5)(NRSV)

Sometimes people talk about "finding" God as if they were seeking a buried treasure that was carefully hidden. God finds us. God knows us first. We may find ourselves already found by God's love. God is closer to us than we are to ourselves and understands us better than we can know ourselves. God comes looking for us when we're lost in confusion. And God keeps looking for us until we discover we've been found by God. Divine grace makes possible even our first steps toward God.

We need to open our eyes. We need to wake up! We need to realize that God is already present in our lives and available for us. We can ask anytime, anywhere. God loves us, heals, invites, inspires, and sends us out to share the good news of who and what we've "found." We need to remove the obstructions that get in the way. We need to remove the distractions, bad habits, and poor substitutes that come between us and God. We may find ourselves already and totally found by God; we may find new life.

?

When have you felt lost? When did you wonder what your next steps should be? Could you find help beyond yourself? Did someone help you? Did you find unexpected clarity or a very helpful opportunity at the right time? Have you found God present with you in a time of uncertainty? How did you know God present? What changed for you?

+

Loving God, be with me constantly and help me know you present. Draw me closer to know you better. Help me listen for you in all places and times. Help me hear you and see you in the others you love. Guide me to use your gifts to understand and choose. Let me shape my actions to follow your call. Loving God, be with me constantly.

Wednesday, 2 Lent

> "Then Peter came to him and asked, 'Lord how often am
> I to forgive my brother if he goes on wronging me? As
> many as seven times?' Jesus replied, 'I do not say seven
> times but seventy times seven.'" (Matt 18:21–22)(REB)

Each season of the year is a wonderful time to forgive, especially
Lent. In the Lord's Prayer we pray that God will forgive us our
sins as we forgive those who sin against us. Forgiveness means we
don't hold the other person in the awkward and painful position of
being in the wrong, less than us, at a disadvantage in the situation.
We don't hold the other person in a ditch of their own making.
We might have to climb into our own ditch to hold them down.
Forgiveness means we don't have to carry the burden of resentment, anger, woundedness. We begin to let it go and start to heal.
We can also remember, as St. Paul reminds us, that "all have sinned
and fall short of the glory of God" (Rom 3:23)(NRSV). We all need
forgiveness, and we know forgiveness best when we share it.

?

Do you "keep score" of another's faults against you? Do these re-
membered faults become a lens for seeing the other in a bad way
or holding them at a distance? Do you seem "more" if they seem
"less"? Are there ways to clear out the barriers between you and
them? Is fault really shared in the situation? Can forgiveness also
be shared?

+

Dear Lord, help us to forgive and be forgiven. Help us move past blame and resentment to reconcile whenever we can. Help us release the obstacles that block your love and inspiration. Help us heal. Let us open the door for your grace.

Thursday, 2 Lent

> "At that time the disciples came to Jesus and asked, 'Who is the greatest in the kingdom of Heaven?' He called a child, set him in front of them, and said, 'Truly I tell you: unless you turn around and become like children, you will never enter the kingdom of Heaven. Whoever humbles himself and becomes like this child will be the greatest in the kingdom of Heaven.'" (Matt 18:1–4)(REB)

The greatest in the kingdom of heaven is definitely *not* the one whose major hope is to be advanced over others. The Son of God shares our humanity in the Incarnation, takes on a state of equality with us, welcomes us as friends. Instead of lording divinity over us, the Son enters our world in vulnerability and humility to share mortal life with its joy and pain. It's the ultimate irony to introduce degrees of greatness or rank in the name of Jesus who brushed aside the separation of God and humanity. Jesus had no rank, no throne, no crown (except a crown of thorns). He never pushed himself ahead of anyone. To follow Jesus is to live with an open heart, filled with wonder, ready for discovery. This joyful freedom is blocked by attachment to a superior position above others or a need to compare, compete, and be superior. It's better to love people than to step over them.

?

Does ambition get in your way? Do you see your future or your advancement when you could see the needs of others around you? Do your agendas get in your way when it's time to help others? Do you get in your own way when you seek God?

+

God of glory, fill our eyes with wonder and our hearts with amazement for you. Holy Lord, brighten our lives with your presence. Draw us near you for healing and hope, guide us for discernment, and strengthen us for service in your name. Help us to see our wholeness and healing are in you. Help us welcome others to share your love instead of pushing them aside.

Friday, 2 Lent

> Jesus said, "Come to me, all who are weary and whose
> load is heavy; I will give you rest. Take my yoke upon you,
> and learn from me, for I am gentle and humble-hearted;
> and you will find rest for your souls. For my yoke is easy
> to wear, my load is light." (Matt 11:28–30)(REB)

Jesus comes to us with love for forgiveness, healing, hope, inspiration, and salvation. He doesn't approach in anger to judge us. We
stand in awe of God, we worship our Lord, but we don't need to
dread a vengeful and threatening god who hurts us. Separation
from God is an infinite loss for us, but it only happens if *we* do the
separating of ourselves from God who loves us. We have free will,
and we can refuse God's offer of love if that's our choice. Divine
love is unbounded, but we need to accept it. The saving love of God
will not be forced down our throats by our Lord.

God welcomes our love and invites our turning around, our
return. The Holy One offers us "comfortable words" of understanding and welcome. God knows our limits and imperfections.
We can bring our heavy burdens to God and set them down. We
can bring God our hurts, our frustrations, and set them down. We
can bring God our pride and set it down. Our Lord invites us to
rest, to heal, and share life that frees us from all the heavy burdens
we've been carrying. We may be surprised to discover how easy it
is to say yes to God and share a life that really lives.

?

Can you turn to God for comfort? Can you express joy, anger, fear,
and other feelings in prayer? Is your relationship with God formal

and distant, or can you say anything on your mind? Can you trust God with your feelings and thoughts, your needs and hopes, your fears and hurts? Can you offer prayers that are simple and direct? Prayers like: *Help! Thanks! What should I do? Amazing!*

+

Dear Lord, speed our prayers like arrows to your heart. Help us always to listen for you as you always hear us. Help us share love and our every concern with you. Help us to trust your love.

Saturday, 2 Lent

"Then one of the scribes, who had been listening to these discussions and had observed how well Jesus answered, came forward and asked him, 'Which is the first of all the commandments?' He answered, 'The first is, 'Hear, O Israel: the Lord our God is the one Lord, and you must love the Lord your God with all your heart, with all your soul, with all your mind, and with all your strength.' The second is this: 'You must love your neighbor as yourself.' No other commandment is greater than these.'" (Mark 12:28–31)(REB)

Jesus said: "Love your enemies; do good to those who hate you; bless those who curse you; pray for those who treat you spitefully." (Luke 6:27–28)(REB)

Who should we love? Jesus invites us to love God, love our friends, love even our enemies, love ourselves. Our different expressions of love for others can be reflections of our love for God. Our different expressions of love for others can also reflect a healthy love for *ourselves*. If we treat ourselves badly, if we neglect to take care of ourselves, if we ignore our own limitations and basic needs, we may find it difficult to care for others. At times we may need to forgive ourselves as well as seeking God's forgiveness and the forgiveness of others. Accepting and celebrating our life as a gift can help us see the giftedness of others and their amazing lives. Facing our challenges, limitations, and mistakes can help us appreciate the struggles of others. Sometimes we may discover a lovable side of a person who seemed difficult, or even a lovable side of ourselves! Love others as you love yourself.

?

Can you remove the obstacles to sharing love? Can you love your neighbor, the people in your world, the people closest to you, the people who need you—as yourself? Can you love yourself? Can you forgive yourself and accept your limitations? Can you accept your gifts and use them well? Can you let yourself be transformed by love?

+

Dear Lord, help us love others as you love us. Help us accept ourselves and others. Uphold us with your love as we reach out for those who need us. Help us find ourselves in you and know your generosity in our love for others.

Sunday, 3 Lent

> Jesus said, "Do not store up for yourselves treasure on earth, where moth and rust destroy, and thieves break in and steal; but store up treasure in heaven, where neither moth nor rust will destroy, nor thieves break in and steal. For where your treasure is, there will your heart be also." (Matt 6:19–21)(REB)

We invest our lives through the way we engage our time, energy, and money. Look at your calendar and check register or purchase histories for hints about your real values as expressed in the "languages" of your activities, energy, and spending. Sometimes we may realize our professed values don't align with our choices, and our treasures have not been invested in the best ways. Lent is a good time for a reality check, and new directions.

?

How do we invest the treasures of our life? Do we live the faith we claim? Are we open to receive God's love and share it? Do we walk the talk? If family and friends are important to us, do we make time for them and care for them? If helping people in need is a priority, do we find ways to make a difference for others? Do we expend ourselves in love? How are your investments? Where is your heart?

+

Loving God, help us give ourselves generously and express our love for you in each decision. Guide us to use our time, energy, and all our resources to share the love in our heart. Let us align our choices with our values. Help us to love generously.

Monday, 3 Lent

Zacchaeus "was eager to see what Jesus looked like; but, being a little man, he could not see him for the crowd. So he ran on ahead and climbed a sycamore tree in order to see him, for he was to pass that way. When Jesus came to the place, he looked up and said, 'Zacchaeus, be quick and come down, for I must stay at your house today.' He climbed down as quickly as he could and welcomed him gladly. At this there was a general murmur of disapproval. 'He has gone in to be the guest of a sinner,' they said. But Zacchaeus stood there and said to the Lord, 'Here and now, sir, I give half my possessions to charity; and if I have defrauded anyone, I will repay him four times over.' Jesus said to him, 'Today salvation has come to this house—for this man too is a son of Abraham.'" (Luke 19: 3–9)(REB)

I suspect Zacchaeus seldom climbed trees and never before gave away much. Jesus' love turned him around. Jesus spotted Zacchaeus in an unexpected place (a tree), and wasn't daunted by his bad history and reputation. Jesus brought salvation to Zacchaeus' house, accepted his hospitality, and found him when he was lost. In a similar way, Jesus can find us when we're lost or confused and bring salvation to our doorstep. His blessing is ours to receive, but we must accept it. It's our choice. And saying yes to Jesus' offer may take us to our own new situations and unexpected places.

?

Do love and faith draw you out of your comfort zone? Do you find yourself active in ways you would never have imagined? As we accept new life in faith by grace, what trees will we climb, what sacrifices will we make, what surprises will we face?

+

Dear Lord, find us in each new day and draw us closer to you. Bless us with forgiveness and inspiration. Give us eyes to see what you have done for us. Help us accept the many second chances you offer us. Help us to turn around. Let us make right what we have done wrong. Let us forgive ourselves. Give us grace to build new lives and be transformed.

Tuesday, 3 Lent

Jesus said, "If you love only those who love you, what credit is that to you? Even sinners love those who love them. Again, if you do good only to those who do good to you, what credit is there in that? Even sinners do as much. And if you lend only where you expect to be repaid, what credit is there in that? Even sinners lend to each other to be repaid in full. But you must love your enemies and do good, and lend without expecting any return, and you will have a rich reward; you will be sons of the Most High, because he himself is kind to the ungrateful and the wicked." (Luke 6:32–36)(REB)

What's in it for me? We can sometimes fall into this attitude in our relationships and decisions. We can be transactional instead of loving, balancing benefit and risk instead of giving ourselves in love. God invites us to show generous love that exceeds prudence. Jesus on the cross wasn't cautious or prudent, but self-giving with ultimate love whatever the cost. He gave everything, sacrificed everything. We are called to give without expectation of return from those we help. There may be no reward or appreciation for what we've done. But Christ's love in us exceeds transactional benefit. Our best life may be reckless abandon into the hands of God, letting go of outcomes and rewards, sharing with others the overflow of God's love in us. Our Lord invites us to treat others better than they deserve, as he treats us.

?

How do you treat the people who don't treat you well? Do you avoid them, ignore them, or fight fire with fire? Have you been able to move a conflict to a better understanding or improve a relationship that has become strained? Where can you start if there's a misunderstanding with another? What do you risk?

+

Blessed are you, O God, our provider and reconciler. You constantly invite us to share your love. Help us make room for all who come near us, including those who are unlike us or dislike us. Help us see you present in everyone, and help us find you in them. Guide us to reconcile and come together. Help us let go of resentments and bias. Let us cherish and protect this world and everyone who shares it with us.

Wednesday, 3 Lent

"And as he sat at dinner in Levi's house, many tax collectors and sinners were also sitting with Jesus and his disciples—for there were many who followed him. When the scribes of the Pharisees saw that he was eating with sinners and tax collectors, they said to his disciples, 'Why does he eat with tax collectors and sinners?' When Jesus heard this, he said to them, 'Those who are well have no need of a physician, but those who are sick; I have come to call not the righteous but sinners.'" (Mark 2:15–17) (NRSV)

There was once an Episcopal parish that didn't want to advertise their Sunday service time in the local newspaper because "the wrong kinds of people" might show up. They were keeping their beloved church community safe and exclusive, like a private club. They were people of faith but not listening to Jesus on this point. He came to heal and save "the wrong kinds of people," and gave his life for them. That is, he gave his life for all of us, to heal and save us all. We're all among "the wrong kind people"—imperfect, limited, fallen, broken, sinners. Lent is a good time to remember who we are and what we aren't. We may discover how much we have in common with the other "wrong kinds of people" in our world. We are all sinners in need of forgiveness, healing, and hope. As St. Paul says, "all have sinned and fall short of the glory of God" (Rom 3:23). The good news is Jesus comes to save us all; and we can share his love with all kinds of people. The door is open.

?

Have you ever been surprised to discover common ground with someone who seemed totally different from you? Did getting to know a person help to change your attitude toward them and others who were like them? Have you ever felt that someone else couldn't see the real you because of prejudice or bias? Could you say or do something to make a difference? Was it possible for the relationship to grow beyond misunderstandings? What can you do to overcome stereotypes? How can you really *see* the person standing in front of you? What helps you to find common ground with another person?

+

All loving God, help us to really *see* the people we meet. Help us move beyond prejudice, stereotypes, and false assumptions. Help us appreciate the diversity of your gifts and love for all. Let us give our best for those who are unlike us, and help us receive from them.

Thursday, 3 Lent

> "Full of the Holy Spirit, Jesus returned from the Jordan, and for forty days he wandered in the wilderness, led by the Spirit and tempted by the devil. During that time he ate nothing, and at the end of it he was famished." (Luke 4:1–2)(REB)

> "Then Jesus, armed with the power of the Spirit, returned to Galilee; and reports about him spread through the whole countryside. He taught in their synagogues and everyone sang his praises." (Luke 4:14–15)(REB)

J. R. R. Tolkien once said in *The Fellowship of the Ring* that all who wander are not lost. Jesus wandered in the wilderness for 40 days after his baptism by John in the River Jordan. During that time he endured temptations by the devil and extreme hunger. This time parallels the 40-year wandering in the wilderness by the people of Israel after their deliverance from Egypt until they finally crossed the River Jordan to enter the Promised Land. Jesus had no particular destination in his wilderness wanderings, but his active public ministry began immediately and powerfully after his sojourn in the wilderness.

In addition to overcoming the devil's three attempts to tempt him with false idols, Jesus had much time to himself. As he wandered there was opportunity to consider the meaning of who he was and his mission in the world. Humanly speaking, he could reflect on his calling, his vocation, and ministry. He could relate his knowledge of God's will to the great possibilities and challenges before him.

Sometimes it helps to wander in an unknown place or mental space when you don't know where you're going. You may see and realize things you didn't expect. If you are lost you may find your way or discover help. You may be surprised by grace and guidance as you wander. Things may become more clear and more possible for you.

?

Do you wander? Can you go beyond your usual habits and thoughts? Can you step beyond what is familiar to you? Will you explore new perspectives and possibilities? Can you be open to God in new ways? Will you allow God to surprise you? Can you try something new that may improve your life? Will this Lent be a time for you to wander?

+

God of our heart and journey, be with us at every step. Share our adventures with us, and let us discover something new. Guide us when we lose our way or become confused. Help us let go of fear. Let us find our way. Draw us nearer to you.

Friday, 3 Lent

> Jesus said, "Nobody lights a lamp and then covers it with a basin or puts it under the bed. You put it on a lampstand so that those who come in may see the light." (Luke 8:16)(REB)

Are there times when you share your faith with others? Can you mention your faith, your practice, your experiences, your story, and the resources of your church or faith community if needed by another person? Sometimes it seems people are more likely to recommend the fine dining of a restaurant, the most exciting sports team they follow or the best movie they've seen, their favorite TV show or vacation destination before giving a clue about the faith that's in them. Years ago the Episcopal Church dedicated our attention to a "Decade of Evangelism," but later some said we needed a previous decade to get ready for a Decade of Evangelism. This isn't about pushing one style of faith or recruiting for one of the sides in an old church controversy. It's about sharing the love of Christ that saves the lost and heals the broken. It's too important to withhold our faith from others because we're so shy or polite we can't share what helps the most in life. We don't have to force anyone into a corner or push our beliefs on them. We can certainly wait for the right time, the right place, and try our best to choose the right words or examples. But the light of Christ in us isn't just for us. Share the light. Help others see.

?

Can you share your faith with someone who needs to hear it? Can you share your faith in a way that leaves room for them to make their own choices? Can you tell how faith has made a difference for you? What has helped you to grow in faith? Who has helped you to move forward in your life of faith? How have they helped you?

+

Lord of our hearts, guide us to share your love and help others to know you better. May we help others to know the hope that moves us forward; let us share the light. Strengthen our faith and help us to reach out to others.

Saturday, 3 Lent

A young man asked Jesus what good deed he must do to
have eternal life. Jesus urged him to keep the commandments. The young man said he had kept all the commandments Jesus mentioned and asked what he lacked.
"Jesus said to him, 'If you wish to be perfect, go, sell
your possessions, and give to the poor, and you will have
treasure in heaven; then come and follow me.' When the
young man heard this, he went away with a heavy heart;
for he was a man of great wealth.'" (Matt 19:21–22)(REB)

We all have choices to make in terms of the lives we live and our
commitments. Sometimes saying yes to one thing means saying
no to something else. Choose well! The young man was enthusi-
astic for the life of faith that Jesus shared, but he was unwilling to
make the necessary sacrifices to follow him. He was tethered. He
couldn't let go of his many possessions to discover a new life of
incredible value and hope. Obeying all the rules wasn't enough. He
couldn't let go of his holdings. He needed a new heart, and a new
set of values in his heart. The choice was his; the choice is ours.

?

What is changing for you during this Lent? Have you taken a step
that makes a difference? Are you still holding back? What changes
do you seek in your life? How can you be generous in living faith?
What will be your new choices during this Lent?

+

Holy God, you love us to the point of sacrifice. Help us to embrace what matters most and let go of whatever blocks your love or hinders our service. Guide us to take the next steps to draw nearer to you. Let us follow you.

Sunday, 4 Lent

> "To his disciples [Jesus] said, 'This is why I tell you not to worry about food to keep you alive or clothes to cover your body. Life is more than food, the body more than clothes. Think of the ravens: they neither sow nor reap; they have no storehouse or barn; yet God feeds them. You are worth far more than the birds! Can anxious thought add a day to your life?'" (Luke 12:22–25)(REB)

I've heard it said that worry is the thief of joy. Worry replaces enjoyment with fretting concern that can't be satisfied by good news or reason. Sometimes worry can be an attempt at control to hold back disruptions or interruptions. It's over-control that gets in the way. The intentions could be good. Someone might worry that a person will be safe, with ongoing worry and concern about everything that could go wrong. The trouble is that good outcomes don't seem to dispel worry for a worrier. If one situation goes well, another cause for worry can quickly appear and the uneasy cycle begins again.

The real answer to worry isn't a white-knuckled resolve to cut it out by an effort of will. The real answer is trust. We can trust God is with us and for us whatever the situation. God is with us, even as we walk through the valley of the shadow of death (Psalm 23:4). We can let go of control, and approach an unknown future with trust and curiosity instead of fear. We don't need an emergency brake to make it all stop so we can regain control. Jesus assures us in the face of every threat that worries us: Fear not, control not, worry not. God whom we have known in the past is with us now and will be there with us in an unknown future.

?

Do you worry? Do you often seem to have something to worry
about? Do fears and worries get more attention from you than they
deserve? Does fear get in the way of doing things you're able to do?
Can you let go of over-control and trust God?

+

Blessed are you, Holy God, who stands with us in all our trials and
challenges. You invite us to let go of fear and all our attempts to
over-control. You invite us to an adventure of faith. Let us find you
present and accept your help. Guide us to approach the unknown
with curiosity instead of fear. Help us to live our lives with trust
in you.

Monday, 4 Lent

Jesus said, "Blessed are the peacemakers; they shall be called God's children." (Matt 5:9)(REB)

Are you a peacemaker? Some people seem to be ready to fight about anything and everything. Politics, religion, the latest controversy in the news, even their favorite sports teams or entertainers. It's possible to invest incredible energy in ongoing arguments that neither side can really win, or in simmering disagreements that have lasted too long. Sometimes all sides continue a cycle of hurting and being hurt that lasts for days, weeks, years, generations.

How to break the cycle? What does it take to be a peacemaker? It may help to see the issue or question from the other side's perspective. It's unlikely one side has all the right answers in any controversy or disagreement. It may help to restate the other's position and check for accuracy. You may be arguing against a position your "opponent" doesn't really share! It may also help to invite the other to restate your position and let you explain if the summary isn't quite right. At least we can listen to each other. We all may learn something. Most importantly, it may be possible to find common ground, an underlying agreement, a shared goal or principle, something both sides can appreciate.

Christians in disagreement love the same Lord, belong to the same body of Christ, and hope for resurrection in the one Christ. This will be life eternal *together* with other members of the one body of Christ—including those who may seem different or difficult. As Miroslav Volf notes, in the final reconciliation enemies will need to become friends. Our current divisions and estrangements are a gash in Christ's body, and a contradiction of our hope that all shall be one in Christ.

Jesus bids us to love our enemies (Matthew 5:44). Loving them, we can be amazed to find the love drawing us together is stronger than whatever tears us apart. Loving our enemies, we can discover they're lovable despite all the differences and disagreements. They may discover the same about us! Together we may be surprised to become friends, and make peace.

?

How do you treat people who disagree with you? How do you treat people who oppose you or make life difficult for you? Do you try to make things hard for them? Do you fight fire with fire, pay back their opposition with more opposition? Were you ever surprised to find much in common with someone who seemed very different from you? Have you ever struggled to get along with an apparent opponent or critic who eventually became a real friend? How can you take the first steps to turn around a difficult or conflicted relationship? How can you make things better for both of you?

+

Draw us together, Lord, bring us together in the arms of your love. Help us to love others as you love them. Guide us to love ourselves as you love us. Surround us with your love. Help us to make peace.

Tuesday, 4 Lent

Jesus said, "Do not judge, and you will not be judged. For as you judge others, so you will yourselves be judged, and whatever measure you deal out to others will be dealt to you. Why do you look at the speck of sawdust in your brother's eye, with never a thought for the plank in your own?" (Matt 7:1–3)(REB)

Be generous. If you want to know the generosity and love of God, share God's love generously with others. Make available God's love for many people in all kinds of situations. We lack generosity when we look down on others, judging them for their apparent short-comings and failures. We have no idea the challenges they have faced and how they have been hurt. It's not our responsibility to sort out fault and blame for them. We can't judge but we may be able to help. The people who need our help don't have to qualify or prove themselves worthy of our attention. Our help is not a *quid pro quo*, a "this for that" kind of transaction where we may weigh benefit and risk. God's generosity leaves all that behind and treats us better than we deserve. We can be generous because we have received abundantly. We can pay our generosity forward, we can pass it on like a blessing that overflows. We may not see the results before our eyes. There may be no thanks or recognition. But we are most truly ourselves, and most completely friends and family of our Lord, when we share God's love.

?

When have you been treated better than you deserved or expected? When have you been surprised by the help you received, or an unexpected second chance? What difference did this make for you? Has another person ever seemed surprised by your generosity? What difference did your help seem to make for them?

+

Dear God, help us to forgive as we have been forgiven by you. Help us to be willing to go extra miles for others as you exceed all expectations for us. Let our love be full and let our hearts be generous. Help us to stop judging others. Guide us to find you present in them.

Wednesday, 4 Lent

> Jesus said, "Ask, and it will be given you; search, and you will find; knock, and the door will be opened for you. For everyone who asks receives, and everyone who searches finds, and for everyone who knocks, the door will be opened." (Matt 7:7–8)(NRSV)

Jesus offers us an invitation and a promise. He invites us to a relationship of love that saves us. This love involves our giving and receiving; and it requires our freedom. Our Lord doesn't force our love or obedience. We get to choose. Real love is given freely, never forced. A thief with a weapon can compel our obedience ("Give me your money or else!"), but never our love ("Love me or else!"). We could have been created perfectly obedient, without capacity to choose or resist—like puppets on a string, or well-programmed computers. But God our creator blesses us with mind and heart and the capacity to choose. Our love—if we choose to give it—will be heartfelt and freely chosen. That would be lost if our obedience were forced by God, and our free response would be destroyed. Our Lord never does that! Instead, Jesus invites and promises. God's love is abundant and always available. Ask and you will receive God's love; knock and the door will open!

?

Do you ask God for help? Are you open to receive it? Does it hurt your pride or make you feel weak to ask for help? Can you ask others for help when you need it? When has accepting help made a difference for you? Can you pay forward the help you have received?

+

Dear God, help us to let go of pride and stubbornness. Let us accept the help we need. Guide us to see that our only completion is in you. Let us share the abundance of your love as we open our hearts to give and receive.

Thursday, 4 Lent

Jesus "entered a certain village, where a woman named Martha welcomed him into her home. She had a sister named Mary, who sat at the Lord's feet and listened to what he was saying. But Martha was distracted by many tasks; so she came to him and asked, 'Lord, do you not care that my sister has left me to do all the work by myself? Tell her to help me.' But the Lord answered her, 'Martha, Martha, you are worried and distracted by many things; there is need of only one thing. Mary has chosen the better part, which will not be taken away from her.'" (Luke 10:38–42)(NRSV)

Have you been distracted lately? It's easy to happen. We're bombarded by demands for our attention. Some of the claims on our time may just be annoying or tiring. Sometimes the biggest threats of distraction can be the "good" demands, the interesting things that seem to reach out and grab us when we need to focus on priorities. Martha wasn't trying to undercut faith or be a distraction. I'm confident she believed she was doing a good thing. After all, she was taking on responsibility, making sure Jesus' visit went well. She just wanted some help from her sister! But Martha lost the meaning of what she was doing in all the details of doing it. As T. S. Eliot says in *Four Quartets*, she had the experience but missed the meaning. Martha let her busy-ness become a potential obstruction for the sharing of love and faith at the heart of Jesus' visit. She would have blocked it for Mary. Get back to work! But Jesus wasn't having it. Don't interrupt his mission in the name of honoring him!

?

Do your favorite projects and agendas get in the way of what matters most in your life? Do you have rationalizations and excuses that provide cover for holding back your love? Can distractions prevent you from being available for the most important moments in your life? Do your routines prevent you from becoming the person you need to be? Do you give your best?

+

God of peace, help us to make room for you in our hearts. Guide us to be still and listen. Help us to find you present in our lives. Let us remove the noise and distractions that get in the way. Surround us with your love. Help us turn to you. Help us to offer our best in love.

Friday, 4 Lent

> "Jesus began to show his disciples that he must go to Jerusalem and undergo great suffering at the hands of the elders and chief priests and scribes, and be killed, and on the third day be raised. And Peter took him aside and began to rebuke him, saying, 'God forbid it, Lord! This must never happen to you.' But he turned and said to Peter, 'Get behind me, Satan! You are a stumbling block to me, for you are setting your mind not on divine things but on human things.'" (Matt 16:21–23)(NRSV)

God's love is freely given to us. We don't have to earn God's love or prove ourselves worthy. God just loves us, forgives us, redeems us, and saves us. God inspires us, sending us forward with vocation and mission. The gift is free, but not cheap. Saying yes to God's love involves us in a new life and changes everything. We may discover new priorities, new ways of being, and some sacrifices as we let go of older patterns and habits that don't serve us. The deeper our acceptance of God's love, the more we embrace the risks of a new way of life with occasions for sacrifice and self-giving.

We learn the way of the cross from Jesus. The cross is never pain for its own sake or punishment from God. We certainly don't need to go looking for sacrifices to make! But sharing God's love will unavoidably involve us in our own sacrifices, as Jesus' sacrifices were essential and integral to his ministry as he faced hard conditions, opposition, and finally death on a cross. It may well be that we do not face a howling mob of opposition or the prospect of being nailed to a wooden cross. But there will be sacrifices and challenges to encounter if we follow the way of love. Maybe we can smile and keep going when we hear an internal voice that warns in a challenging time, "God forbid! This must never happen to you!"

?

What has the cross meant to you? What sacrifices have you accepted in your life? How have your sacrifices been an expression of love? How is your life being changed by your sacrifices? Have your sacrifices helped you to turn around in faith? Have you made any sacrifices this Lent, large or small? What have you taken on or let go?

+

Dear Lord, you offer yourself for us and give us everything. Surround us with your love. Guide us to sacrifice for the better part that matters the most. Let us take up our cross and follow you. Let us share new life.

Saturday, 4 Lent

"As Jesus passed along the Sea of Galilee, he saw Simon and his brother Andrew casting a net into the sea—for they were fishermen. And Jesus said to them, 'Follow me and I will make you fish for people.' And immediately they left their nets and followed him. As he went a little further, he saw James son of Zebedee and his brother John, who were in their boat mending the nets. Immediately he called them, and they left their father Zebedee in the boat with the hired men, and followed him." (Mark 1:16–20)(NRSV)

"As Jesus was walking along he saw a man called Matthew sitting at the tax booth; and he said to him, 'Follow me.' And he got up and followed him." (Matt 9:9)(NRSV)

Jesus invites Peter and Andrew, James and John, and Matthew to follow him—and they do. They make a change, they begin new lives, they trust Jesus. They have no idea where they're going with him that day or what they will do in the future. They have no idea how things will turn out. There will be risk. We know it won't be safe for many of them, but it will be their amazing ministry shared with Jesus and continued by them in his name.

A disciple is a follower. The disciples left their former lives and began their vocation of following Jesus without hesitation. That was an enormous first step for them, as it is for us as Christians. We follow Jesus' way of love that is the way of the cross. It's our adventure of faith.

?

Does God invite you to follow? Does God invite you to change? How do you respond? Where has it taken you? Where are you headed? How does faith change your direction? What is changing for you now?

+

Holy God, loving guide of our souls, always draw us nearer to you. Ask and we will follow. Let us share your life and love. Help us see we're most ourselves when we live in you. Show us the way.

Sunday, 5 Lent

> Jesus said, "Do not think that I have come to abolish the law or the prophets; I have come not to abolish but to fulfill." (Matt 5:17)(NRSV)

> Jesus said, "You have heard that it was said, 'You shall love your neighbor and hate your enemy.' But I say to you, Love your enemies and pray for those who persecute you." (Matt 5:43)(NRSV)

Jesus fulfills the law and the prophets with love. If we love our neighbor we will not tell lies about our neighbor, we will not steal from our neighbor, we will not kill our neighbor. And our loving treatment of the neighbor is not just to avoid getting in trouble or escape the law's condemnation. We love the neighbor for their sake and ours. Loving the neighbor we love God more, especially if the neighbor is in need. In this way we fulfill the great commandment to love God with all our heart, soul, and mind; and to love our neighbor as we love ourselves (Mark 12:30–31). And our neighbor isn't just the person living next door or down the block. Our neighbor is literally anyone in our life, anyone coming to our attention, every stranger and random person—even an enemy. Our choice to love and not hate an enemy may help them see us differently, or see life differently. Maybe we will learn from that person in ways no one else can offer or make possible.

?

What have you done today that expresses love for someone you love, a friend, a stranger, a person in need? What is the best expression of love you have ever given or received? What is the best expression of love you have ever witnessed? How can you share love today?

+

Blessed are you, Lord God, lover of souls, you draw us near to your heart and give us much to share. We know your love in loving others, loving the ones you love so dearly, loving all. Help us to use the gifts you give us. Help us to find your love in us and share it.

Monday, 5 Lent

> Jesus said, "The kingdom of heaven is like treasure hidden in a field, which someone found and hid, then in his joy he goes and sells all that he has and buys that field. Again, the kingdom of heaven is like a merchant in search of fine pearls; on finding one pearl of great value, he went and sold all that he had and bought it." (Matt 13:44–46)(NRSV)

What are your priorities? What comes first for you? Sometimes saying a real *yes* to one possibility means saying *no* to many other possibilities. A necessary sacrifice comes with many choices we make. The fishermen who followed Jesus left behind their family, the family fishing business, and familiar surroundings. They left behind a world where they basically knew what to expect on a daily basis. Following Jesus was for them a real sacrifice. It was, as Dietrich Bonhoeffer says, costly grace.

Sometimes we find a choice worth making, a choice surpassing all the others, a "pearl" worth everything we can offer and whatever it takes to be our own. This all begins with the life of God in us, the love of God who forgives and saves us, the Spirit of God who moves us and sends us with mission. Accepting divine grace will lead us to give back love with all we have. We sort out the specifics of our ministry and self-offering as we encounter situations that call in particular ways for our generosity and sacrifices.

?

What are the choices you face? How will you share your love? What are your priorities? Where do you find the "pearl" that matters most? What will you give for it? What will you sacrifice for it? How does your search for the pearl draw you into new life?

+

Dear God, help us to give our best in loving you. Guide us to see beyond our own needs and agendas. Help us sacrifice for what matters the most. Let us find the pearl of life in you. Be with us as we make a new beginning.

Tuesday, 5 Lent

Jesus said, "I am the good shepherd. The good shepherd lays down his life for the sheep. The hired hand, who is not the shepherd and does not own the sheep, sees the wolf coming and leaves the sheep and runs away—and the wolf snatches them and scatters them. The hired hand runs away because a hired hand does not care for the sheep. I am the good shepherd. I know my own and my own know me, just as the Father knows me and I know the Father. And I lay down my life for the sheep." (John 10:11–15)(NRSV)

Jesus "told them this parable: 'Which one of you, having a hundred sheep and losing one of them, does not leave the ninety-nine in the wilderness and go after the one that is lost until he finds it? When he has found it, he lays it on his shoulders and rejoices. And when he comes home, he calls together his friends and neighbors, saying to them, 'Rejoice with me, for I have found my sheep that was lost.'" (Luke 15:3–6)(NRSV)

Jesus embraces the generosity, persistence, love, and risk of his calling and describes this life in terms of being the good shepherd. Unlike the hired hand, the good shepherd cares for the sheep. Unlike the hired hand, the good shepherd stands by the sheep when they are threatened. The good shepherd risks his life for the sheep; he lays down his life for the sheep when necessary. Unlike the hired hand, the good shepherd knows the sheep and the sheep know him. Many pet owners can describe very close relationships with their animals; they know each other well. The sheep of the good shepherd are not just livestock, not just a herd. Each one matters;

the good shepherd knows each one. The good shepherd will seek out and find any one of the sheep if they stray and get lost. He will joyfully carry the lost sheep home on his shoulders.

The parable of the good shepherd points us to a way of life that cares for others. We take time to know the people in our world and their stories. We build relationships with people instead of using them as objects for our purposes. We stand by them in times of threat, hurt, or loss; we help them find their way forward when uncertain or confused. We risk ourselves in the vulnerability of love.

?

How can we *be* the good shepherd, the good spouse, the good relative, the good friend, the good neighbor, the good colleague? Can you seek the other when lost or hurting? Can you go out of your way to help? Can you risk? Can you stand with the other in a time of danger or threat? Can you provide a safe place for them? Can you help them find their way home?

+

O, good Shepherd, be my guard and guide. Lead me beside still waters. Guide me along right pathways. Be with me and comfort me. Strengthen me in the face of every evil. Sustain me in every danger. Help me to know your abundance. May your love overflow. Bring me home.

Wednesday, 5 Lent

Jesus prayed concerning his disciples, "Sanctify them in the truth; your word is truth. As you have sent me into the world, so I have sent them into the world. And for their sakes I sanctify myself, so that they also may be sanctified in truth. I ask not only on behalf of these, but also on behalf of those who will believe in me through their word, that they may all be one. As you, Father, are in me and I am in you, may they also be in us, so that the world may believe that you have sent me. The glory that you have given me I have given them, so that they may be one, as we are one." (John 17:17–22)(NRSV)

The Christ who enters this world to save us also draws us together. Christ shares the loving union of Son with Father, making the divine life and glory of God available to us. This saving union of love isn't just ours to keep to ourselves like a private property or secret. We learn of God through others, we best know the love of God with others, we share the love of God for others in community and relationships. We offer what we have received and tell what we know. It's important to remove the barriers that make it harder for us to know God together. It's important in our lives and communities to focus on the love that saves us, avoiding distractions and needless tangents that get in the way. We're better together. Lent is a good time to identify and remove obstacles to sharing faith and being one in Christ. God's love drawing us together is stronger than all our divisions.

?

How can we build bridges with those who seem so different from us? How do we find common ground? What draws us together? Can we disagree at times and still walk together?

+

God of love and hope, draw us together in your arms. Surround us with your love. Help us see that we are all one in you and need each other. Strengthen us to honor our differences and not be estranged by them. Let us be complete in you.

Thursday, 5 Lent

> Jesus said, "The kingdom of God is as if someone would scatter seed on the ground, and would sleep and rise night and day, and the seed would sprout and grow, he does not know how. The earth produces of itself, first the stalk, then the head, then the full grain in the head. But when the grain is ripe, at once he goes in with his sickle, because the harvest has come." (Mark 4:26–29)(NRSV)

The kingdom of heaven doesn't work on our timetable or expectations; it is certainly beyond our control. Many look for definitive proofs, clear evidence, favorable outcomes. It seems only fair that our goodness will be quickly rewarded and our goals promptly fulfilled. We want visible results! Instead, we can discover the kingdom of God has been active in ways we could not recognize, like planted seeds active below the surface of the ground. Who knows when the first green sprouts will appear? Who knows the day or the hour? This new life is invisible to us in its first stages, and its pace is unpredictable. It may be out of our control, but it's vibrant.

The kingdom of God is a mystery beyond our knowing, even as we are included in its life, participate in its growth, and discern it near us. The kingdom of God moves on God's time, not ours. The next moment in the unfolding kingdom may happen in an aeon of human history or the blink of an eye. It's beyond our measurements and calculations; it's beyond us. We do well to offer our love and share our faith as we release our impatient deadlines for the kingdom of God. Be ready! The instant to invite, encourage, welcome, console, heal, prepare, or send others may arise when least expected. It's the next movement of the kingdom, an ongoing harvest we share in God's time.

?

Do you get impatient? Are you frustrated when the timing of an activity is out of your control? Have you discovered a wonderful process was moving forward without any signs of progress that you could see? Have outcomes or results taken shapes you didn't anticipate? Has God's activity in your life been an unexpected gift for you? How?

+

Dear God, your love is astounding and full of surprises. You come like the wind, surrounding us with care in ways we can't explain or predict. Open the doors of opportunity for us to know you better and spread your kingdom. Open our eyes to see you present in most unexpected ways. Help us let go of control that demands our own terms and timetables. Guide us into the uncharted adventure of life with you.

Friday, 5 Lent

Jesus "came to his own hometown, and his disciples followed him. On the sabbath he began to teach in the synagogue, and many who heard him were astounded. They said, 'Where did this man get all this? What is this wisdom that has been given to him? What deeds of power are being done by his hands! Is not this the carpenter, the son of Mary and brother of James and Joses and Judas and Simon, and are not his sisters here with us?' And they took offense at him. Then Jesus said to them, 'Prophets are not without honor, except in their hometown, and among their own kin, and in their own house.' And he could do no deed of power there, except that he laid his hands on a few sick people and cured them. And he was amazed at their unbelief." (Mark 6:1–6)(NRSV)

Have you ever felt limited by others' low expectations? It went that way for Jesus when he visited his own hometown. "He could do no deed of power there." People thought they had him pegged. He was the carpenter, and they knew all his relatives. They thought they knew just where he fit in their society. But they couldn't *see* Jesus; they couldn't believe. Jesus was not distracted by the poor reception he received. He knew his own truth and identity. He healed some in that place and continued his ministry elsewhere to heal and save many others.

Following Jesus is a risky way to live. Following him we find ourselves drawn out of our places of comfort into a way of generous love that is vulnerable, not always understood or appreciated, limited at times by others' expectations, sometimes resisted or even attacked. And yet by grace we can find our way forward, knowing who we are and whose we are. We can love, give, and risk.

?

Has faith ever drawn you out of your comfort zone? Has your life of faith at times meant taking risks or being vulnerable? Have you resisted or held back from fully engaging your faith? Did you worry about what others would think, or how you might seem different from others? Were you embarrassed by your faith? Have you felt limited by others' low expectations? What helped you to know and live your truth?

+

Dear Lord, draw us into the way of love. Guide us to hear your call. Help us take up our cross and follow you. Remind us not to be afraid because we are safe in you. Strengthen us to face resistance and praise without losing sight of you. Walk with us.

Saturday, 5 Lent

> After Jesus freed the man from the unclean spirits, people "came to Jesus and saw the demoniac sitting there, clothed and in his right mind, the very man who had had the legion; and they were afraid." As Jesus was getting into the boat to leave, "the man who had been possessed by demons begged him that he might be with him. But Jesus refused, and said to him, 'Go home to your friends, and tell them how much the Lord has done for you, and what mercy he has shown you.' And he went away and began to proclaim in the Decapolis how much Jesus had done for him; and everyone was amazed." (Mark 5:15, 18–20)(NRSV)

The man was fully clothed and in his right mind after Jesus freed him from the unclean spirits. Jesus directed him to return home to his friends and give witness to the healing mercy he received. He proclaimed this good news publicly in the Decapolis. Luke's narrative of this story tells us that afterwards the man "went away, proclaiming throughout the city how much Jesus had done for him." (Luke 8:39)(NRSV)

The gospel tells us no more about what happened later in the life of this man who once lived naked among the tombs and broke the chains and shackles that were meant to subdue him. What a challenge it must have been for him and the people who knew him when he returned! Instead of howling on the mountains he proclaimed in the city everything Jesus had done for him. Did his neighbors listen to him? Did they open their doors for him, help him find a place to live and work in the city, accept him as one of their own? Could he join their society? Could he be their friend? Could he marry a member of their family?

At the heart of Christian faith and especially Lent is the place of forgiveness, conversion, healing, new life and possibility. This is our turning around by grace, and it is an ongoing process of growth and renewal in faith. Christ's life in us will change us; we discover new life in him. As we change, our relationships will change. We may become more generous, loving, forgiving, available.

As we change for the better it will be helpful if others welcome our changes instead of insisting we continue to be the person they remember. In the same way, we can make room for the changed lives and healing improvements we find in others. We can encourage them to keep moving forward as they continue to surprise us. At some point the neighbors of the healed man needed to let go their reminders of his past and welcome the new man who lived among them. We can do the same.

?

Do you need to forgive someone? Do you need to receive forgiveness from someone? Do you feel stuck in the past concerning something bad that happened? Can you let go of the hurt you feel? Can you undo or apologize for the harm you caused? Can you forgive as you have been forgiven by God? Can you accept another's forgiveness? Can you forgive yourself? Have you ever celebrated reconciliation?

+

Merciful God, you restore us to life in its fullness by your forgiveness and love. Help us remove all barriers that separate us from you and each other. Let us forgive generously as you forgive us. Let us accept forgiveness with humility. Guide us to let go of old hurts and resentments. Help us to build a new life in love. Help us to welcome the healing changes we find in others.

The Sunday of the Passion: Palm Sunday

"The crowds that went ahead of Jesus and that followed were shouting 'Hosanna to the Son of David! Blessed is the one who comes in the name of the Lord! Hosanna in the highest heaven!' When he entered Jerusalem, the whole city was in turmoil, asking, 'Who is this?' The crowds were saying, 'This is the prophet Jesus from Nazareth in Galilee.'" (Matt 21:8–11)(NRSV)

"Now the chief priests and the elders persuaded the crowds to ask for Barabbas and to have Jesus killed. The governor again said to them, 'Which of the two do you want me to release for you?' And they said, 'Barabbas.' Pilate said to them, 'Then what should I do with Jesus who is called the Messiah?' All of them said, 'Let him be crucified!' Then he asked, 'Why, what evil has he done?' But they shouted all the more, 'Let him be crucified!'" (Matt 27:20–23)(NRSV)

The crowd in Jerusalem was fickle. It seems likely that some in the crowd who screamed for Jesus' execution were among those who sang his praises at his triumphal entry into Jerusalem. Those of us who participate fully in the Palm Sunday/Passion Sunday liturgy may also feel awkward and ill as we first sing Hosannas to the Son of David at the Liturgy of the Palms and then cry "Away with him! Away with him! Crucify him!" during the Passion Gospel. The perspective of the crowd can change quickly.

?

Do you follow the crowd? Do you bend to peer pressure? Are you fickle? Do you wait to see the most popular position before declaring yourself? Can you take a minority position that seems most true but also unpopular? Will you protect another's right to hold a minority position even if you disagree? Will you defend a person with no defender when everyone else has decided against them? Can you speak against gossip? In the ongoing drama of Jesus' Passion, do you stand by him? Or do you follow the crowd?

+

Dear Lord, be present with us in all the times of our lives, when we feel strong and when we falter. Help us to be true in our love for you when it is easy and when it is difficult. Let us be without fear or self-consciousness as we bear witness to our faith. Strengthen us to stand up for others when needed as we stand close to you. Help us speak for those who have no voice. Guide us not to bend to harmful peer pressure. Accept our constant love.

Monday in Holy Week

Jesus said to the disciples, "'You will all become deserters because of me this night; for it is written, "I will strike the shepherd, and the sheep of the flock will be scattered." . . . .

"Peter said to Jesus, 'Though all become deserters because of you, I will never desert you.' Jesus said to him, 'Truly I tell you, this very night, before the cock crows, you will deny me three times.'" (Matt 26:31, 33–34) (NRSV)

"Now Peter was sitting outside in the courtyard. A servant-girl came to him and said, 'You also were with Jesus the Galilean.' But he denied it before all of them, saying, 'I do not know what you are talking about.' When he went out to the porch, another servant-girl saw him, and she said to the bystanders, 'This man was with Jesus of Nazareth.' Again, he denied it with an oath, 'I do not know the man.' After a little while the bystanders came up and said to Peter, 'Certainly you are also one of them, for your accent betrays you.' Then he began to curse, and he swore an oath, 'I do not know the man!' At that moment the cock crowed." (Matt 26:69–74)(NRSV)

Peter was an enthusiast, and deeply loyal to Jesus. He was the first to identify Jesus as "the Messiah, the Son of the living God" (Matt 16:16)(NRSV). Peter was deeply devoted to Jesus his Lord, and promised never to desert him. And yet Peter denied Jesus three times when confronted after Jesus' arrest. Unlike Judas, this was an unplanned betrayal of Jesus and the relationship Peter shared with him. It happened at a fearful time of stress and uncertainty. Unlike

Judas, Peter would know himself to be forgiven and return again to share the faith he knew with Jesus. This was not the end for Peter or his ministry. He lived to fulfill his promise.

?

Have you fallen short in a time of stress or confusion? Have you failed to fulfill promises you confidently made? In the ongoing drama of Jesus' Passion, have you lived the role of Peter? Can you, like Peter, accept God's forgiveness and forgive yourself? Can you continue faithfully to seek fulfilment of the promises you made and the gifts you have received?

+

Loving and gracious Lord, help us know your forgiveness and deep understanding of all we have done and all we have failed to do. Your love is constant and our shortcomings are all washed clean in you. Give us your hand. Help us stand when we fall. Help us start over when we might otherwise despair and give up. Help us forgive ourselves as you forgive us. Guide us to turn around and embrace you. Renew us in your love.

Tuesday in Holy Week

"One of the twelve, who was called Judas Iscariot, went to the chief priests and said, 'What will you give me if I betray Jesus to you?' They paid him thirty pieces of silver. And from that moment he began to look for an opportunity to betray him." (Matt 26:14–16)(NRSV)

"While Jesus was still speaking, Judas, one of the twelve, arrived; with him was a large crowd with swords and clubs, from the chief priests and the elders of the people. Now the betrayer had given them a sign, saying, 'The one I will kiss is the man; arrest him.' At once he came up to Jesus and said, 'Greetings, Rabbi!' and kissed him. Jesus said to him, 'Friend, do what you are here to do.'" (Matt 26:47–50)(NRSV)

Judas is aptly named "the betrayer" by the Gospel. He makes a show of respect and affection when he encounters Jesus at Gethsemane, but it's a calculated betrayal and a performed lie. Jesus cuts through the fake, tells Judas to do what he intends, and yet calls him friend. There's no attack from Jesus, no striking back at the one who planned to hurt him. But Judas, the betrayer and false disciple, contradicted himself.

We undermine ourselves when our actions contradict our words. Without integrity of belief and actions we divide ourselves against ourselves and betray trust. We fall; we cannot stand. We cannot be believed or trusted. We isolate ourselves in a horrible aloneness. We undermine ourselves with lies. But forgiveness is still available to us, as it was for Judas. We can still turn around and live with integrity. We can make a new start.

?

Have you betrayed? Have your actions contradicted your words and identity? Have you failed others who counted on you? How did it feel? In the ongoing drama of Jesus' Passion, have you lived the role of Judas? How can you turn around the situation? Can you begin to stand after a fall? Can you accept the forgiveness and help that is available? Can you stand with our Lord?

+

Merciful God, help us turn around our failures. Guide us to do what we can to make things right and undo the harm we have caused. Help us to accept forgiveness as we forgive those who have hurt us. Let us build a new life. Draw us nearer to you in this new day. Be our light in the darkness, the hope in our despair. Surprise us with joy and new direction. Help us to live and love.

Wednesday in Holy Week

"The stone that the builders rejected has become the chief cornerstone. This is the Lord's doing; it is marvelous in our eyes." (Ps 118:22–23)(NRSV)

The landowner of the vineyard sent his slaves to the tenants to collect his produce at harvest time. "But the tenants seized his slaves and beat one, killed another, and stoned another. Again he sent other slaves, more than the first; and they treated them in the same way. Finally he sent his son to them, saying, 'They will respect my son.' But when the tenants saw the son, they said to themselves, 'This is the heir; come, let us kill him and get his inheritance.' So they seized him, threw him out of the vineyard, and killed him. Now when the owner of the vineyard comes, what will he do to those tenants?' They said to him, 'He will put those wretches to a miserable death, and lease the vineyard to other tenants who will give him the produce at the harvest time.' Jesus said to them, 'Have you never read in the scriptures: 'The stone that the builders rejected has become the cornerstone; this was the Lord's doing, and it is amazing in our eyes'"? (Matt 21:35–42)(NRSV)

Jesus' parable of the vineyard and the wicked tenants is a painfully accurate foretelling of his own sacrifice and glory. The rejected stone becomes the chief cornerstone and it is marvelous in our eyes. The cross was not for Jesus the sad and tragic ending of the career of a promising religious leader. The cross was for him and us the entry to resurrection life sharing the eternal love and glory of God.

Sometimes an apparent failure or rejection can be the threshold to unimagined opportunities and acceptance. Initial appearances can be deceptive relative to ultimate outcomes. The best may come out of the worst. We can be most open to help and realize that God is near when we feel lost and broken. Jesus shares with us the pain of rejection and the hope of redemption. Today's failure or rejection may be reshaped into a new and larger repurposing of our life that will amaze us. We can turn around.

?

Have you ever felt rejected, excluded, unwanted? Did it leave you feeling broken? Was it possible for that hard time to become the beginning of something new and good? Have you ever needed to pass through the rejection or misunderstanding of others to do something very important? Was their response painful to you? What helped you to keep going? Could you find help and engage your faith when you most needed it? Who helped?

+

Lord of the cross, Lord of glory, be with us in all our struggles. Give us light in the dark; give us hope in despair. Give us healing and hope when we are broken. Help us see that our broken pieces can take a new shape and completion. Help us find redemption in you.

Maundy Thursday

"After washing their feet Jesus put on his garment and sat down again. 'Do you understand what I have done for you?' he asked 'You call me Teacher and Lord, and rightly so, for that is what I am. Then if I, your Lord and Teacher, have washed your feet, you also ought to wash one another's feet. I have set you an example: you are to do as I have done for you." (John 13:12–15)(REB)

"I received from the Lord what I also handed on to you, that the Lord Jesus on the night when he was betrayed took a loaf of bread, and when he had given thanks, he broke it and said, 'This is my body that is for you. Do this in remembrance of me.' In the same way he took the cup also, after supper, saying, 'This cup is the new covenant in my blood. Do this, as often as you drink it, in remembrance of me.' For as often as you eat this bread and drink the cup, you proclaim the Lord's death until he comes." (1 Cor 11:23–26)(NRSV)

Do this, Jesus says. Share the blessed bread and wine that he identifies with his very life, his body and blood. His disciples share the Last Supper with Jesus as he offers himself for our salvation. He provides a way to re-engage his loving death and victorious life for all time. Do this, Jesus says. It's his "new commandment": Love one another (John 13:34). Wash each other's feet. Serve others with humility. Share the love and life we receive from God. Know the fullness of joy we're meant for and the love that completes us; know God's love more deeply as you share it more fully and widely with others. We may be surprised by the abundance of God's love in us.

Jesus "knew that his hour had come to depart from this world and go to the Father" when he shared the Last Supper with his disciples and washed their feet (John 13:1)(NRSV). Jesus would be arrested in a matter of hours and executed the next afternoon. In the face of threats and danger, Jesus' direction for his disciples was for them to serve humbly, love generously, and remember him.

?

How do you serve humbly and love generously? How do you remember Jesus? Can you share his sacrifice? Can you drink his cup? Can you wash another's feet? Can you proclaim Jesus in your life? Can you share the bread of life?

+

Most humble Lord, you bent down to wash the disciples' feet before you were lifted on the cross and raised in glory. Help us to know you present as we love and serve others. Let our hands continue your works of mercy and grace in the world. Dear Lord, you offered yourself in love by sharing bread and wine before offering yourself on the cross. Help us to find new ways in each day to know and share your love with others. Help us remember that your breaking of bread also means the breaking of death, the breaking of pride, the breaking of isolation and estrangement, the breaking of despair. Be known to us, Lord, in the breaking of bread.

Good Friday

"From noon on, darkness came over the whole land until three in the afternoon. And about three o'clock Jesus
cried with a loud voice, 'Eli, Eli, lema sabachthani?' that
is, 'My God, my God, why have you forsaken me?'" (Matt
27:45–46)(NRSV)

"My God, my God, why have you forsaken me? Why are
you so far from helping me, from the words of my groan-
ing? O my God, I cry by day, but you do not answer; and
by night, but find no rest." (Ps 22:1–2)(NRSV)

Jesus' cry of despair and abandonment from the cross is heartrend-
ing. He experiences separation, isolation, brokenness. His suffer-
ing is extreme. There is no reprieve; the brutal end is inevitable.
And yet the psalm he chooses for his lament is itself an expression
of deep hope in the divine triumph. Psalm 22, like other psalms of
lament (e.g., Pss 3, 13, 54, 55, 56, 59, 69), moves from expressions
of anguish to praise and thanksgiving for God. Psalm 22 moves
from a forsaken cry of great despair to deep confidence, hope, and
praise for God: "Posterity will serve him; future generations will be
told about the Lord, and proclaim his deliverance to a people yet
unborn, saying that he has done it" (Ps 22:30–31)(NRSV). Jesus
chose to express his lament in the words of Psalm 22, and he knew
well the hopeful resolution of that psalm.

It's good to express our feelings of helplessness and be open to
help. It's also good to remember there is no divine abandoning, despite great pain and loss in the moment. Jesus was never for a moment outside the Father's love, even in his darkest and most fearful

times, despite the worst appearances. He knew where Psalm 22 would lead. He knew where God's love would be. So do we.

?

Are there times when you have felt abandonned, lost, hopeless? Have you been surprised by unexpected help or a way to move forward when there seemed to be no hope in the situation? Did a door open when everything seemed to be closed to you? Have you discovered God present with you in surprising ways or circumstances? Have you been able to help someone else when they felt hopeless or lost?

+

Dear Lord, help us find you present in our times of struggle and pain. Always be with us. Brighten our darkness and calm our fear. Guide us to know you never forsake us; you never forget us. Your love endures. Stand with us always. Help us to take up our cross and follow you. Let us share your love.

Holy Saturday

> "Joseph of Arimathea, who was a disciple of Jesus, though a secret one because of his fear of the Jews, asked Pilate to let him take away the body of Jesus. Pilate gave him permission; so he came and removed his body. Nicodemus, who had at first come to Jesus by night, also came, bringing a mixture of myrrh and aloes, weighing about a hundred pounds. They took the body of Jesus and wrapped it with the spices of linen cloths, according to the burial custom of the Jews. Now there was a garden in the place where he was crucified, and in the garden there was a new tomb in which no one had ever been laid. And so, because it was the Jewish day of Preparation, and the tomb was nearby, they laid Jesus there."
> (John 19:38–42)(NRSV)

Joseph of Arimathea and Nicodemus each went public after Jesus' death on the cross. Joseph was a secret disciple of Jesus, and Nicodemus came to Jesus in the dark to ask questions of faith. Stepping out of the darkness could have been a dangerous move for both of them at that time. The forces that killed Jesus could easily have harmed them. The disciples weren't around. But Joseph and Nicodemus found new courage to make public their connection with Jesus. They stepped forward.

Sometimes Christians can be shy about their faith. We can rationalize that it's a private matter, to each their own. But we can find times when we are strongly called and deeply moved to put our faith into visible, tangible expression. Joseph and Nicodemus honored Jesus' body after his death, and gave witness with their lives.

?

In the ongoing drama of Jesus' Passion, can you live the role of Joseph or Nicodemus? Can you step forward to help and give witness? Can you go public with your faith? What holds you back? Is your faith hidden? Are you shy about your faith? Can you be a witness of faith before others? Do your actions reflect your faith?

+

Holy God, stir our hearts and let us show your love in our lives. Strengthen us to risk; help us share the life that saves. Guide us to help others as we have been helped. Let us be vulnerable and take up our cross to follow you. Help us let go of everything that holds us back, everything that comes between us and your love. Help us always to turn around and embrace your love. Let us celebrate new life in you.